# The 15 Fundamental Laws of De- Escalation

How to Put Out Fires, Not Start Them

**Brendan King**

**The 15 Fundamental Laws of De- Escalation
How to Put Out Fires, Not Start Them**

© 2020 by Brendan King All Rights Reserved

All Rights Reserved. No part of this publication may be reproduced, stored in a retrieval system, or transmitted in any form or by any means without the express written consent of the copyright holder.

**Preface**

In the early years of working in mental health and crisis prone workplace environments, I was repeatedly taught (*and had come to believe*) that learning the right thing to say, using the right language, or having the right "*process*" during a crisis was the most important factor. For this reason, I attempted to soak up and learn as many de-escalation "techniques" as I could. I watched the pro's that I worked with. I studied their interactions and the responses of the individuals they were dealing with. I listened to every nuance in their tone of voice, their inflections, and their body language. I read their debriefs. I asked questions. I truly did everything I could to emulate them and what I thought they did. I strived to be the best de-escalator in the whole hospital.

Years later, in line with those experiences and that mindset, I wrote my first book, "**Calm Every Storm – Preventing Aggressive Behavior with Your Words**", as a collection of over 80+ tips and techniques for de-escalation. They are unique and helpful in providing the reader with strategies that can be utilized right away to mitigate challenging situations. Many readers of the book have found it to be very helpful and have actually taken the time to reach out to me and let me know that they have used the methods during some very hostile and threatening situations. I am surely happy to hear that.

Our training curriculum that I developed with the help of a few key individuals on my team, has also served to empower over 350,000 people at the time of this writing.* I know it has had a wonderful impact on helping to "calm the world down" and lessen the intensity of crisis situations many responders face. Our physical intervention / passive restraint system has been utilized in 39 states, and internationally with great success. At the time of this writing*, with over 15 years of use, there have been no sentinel events (deaths) or major injuries associated with our techniques. I am confident that will remain the case in the future as well. Our proprietary physical intervention technique, taught to be utilized when facing imminent danger is one of, if not the most effective method taught in the industry to mitigate violent behavior, hands down.

Even with all these fantastic, exciting, and positive results, I have always felt like "*techniques*" were truly not the total solution. I have continued to see persons who have also been taught the "*techniques*" struggle as I have at times during simple, or complex crisis situations. I have witnessed the struggle to master the "*art*" of communication, and the failure to connect and engage with the individual in crisis. I have felt for many recent years that there was far *more* to de-escalation than what I had experienced thus far. *4/20/2020

Nearly two decades later, having the opportunity to train all over the country and internationally, speaking to thousands of people in nearly every type of workplace, with all levels of experience and backgrounds, I have come to know and realize that having the right **skill set** is only a *part* of successful de-escalation, not the whole.

I know that the majority of crisis intervention and de-escalation programs in the industry continue to focus nearly 100% on the behavior and mindset of the individual in crisis, vs. being laser focused on the behavior and mindset of the **RESPONDER**. This is the downfall of the current de-escalation training industry. Instead of focusing on a particular word, phrase, technique, method, process, etc. the focus needs to be on the responder themselves and the fundamental "*laws*" of de-escalation.

To put it more clearly and use a short analogy; A toilet plunger is a very handy and effective tool, when you know how to use it properly. If you do not use it properly, with the right amount of pressure, the right angle, the right timing, you can end up very quickly making a huge mess and standing in a puddle of feces.

Similar to a crisis situation, you may have the right de-escalation techniques, but without the right *mindset*, the right "*footing*", the right philosophy, or understanding of the fundamental "*laws*", you will likely create a far "*shittier*" situation, and fail to resolve the issue at all.

Plumbers are expensive. Why? Because they get into the shittiest situations that no one else wants to deal with, and they fix it. Most of us will not desire to join the plumber in his work, nor will we even want to watch. We are disgusted, feel embarrassed and uncomfortable with the situation as a whole, and are not truly prepared for what that plumber has to deal with. That plumber though, is happy. To start with, they come into your house with the right **mindset**. They have the right boots. They have the right gloves. They carry the right tools, and recognize the importance of what they are doing, the success or "*money*" they will make, and know it's up to them to fix it. They know how valuable and needed they are, at that exact moment. Yes, that is the goal of this book. I want to help you to be the best dang de-escalation "*plumber*" there is.

Thank you for taking the time to read this book, I do believe wholeheartedly that if we all can remember these fundamentals before, during, and after the next crisis we face, we can truly change the world, and be a part of helping to calm it down, and continue to "*Calm Every Storm*"

Change lives,

Brendan King

CEO and Founder

Crisis Consultant Group, Inc

www.crisisconsultantgroup.com

**Law 1:**
Care More Than Others Deserve

---

John Maxwell is well known to have said "*People don't care how much you know, until they know how much you care*". I believe this is the most important determining factor related to your ability to de-escalate a person in crisis.

Period, end of story.

Demonstrating genuine care and concern for another human being in crisis is not always easy. For some, this comes naturally. For others this is nearly impossible. For the majority, if we remember to focus on it, and pay attention to it, and apply it to every word and action that leaves our body when responding, we will be very likely to successfully resolve a challenging situation. What exactly does it take to "*care more than others deserve*"? This requires a number of skills, focused beliefs, and surely the right attitude.

When considering skills; first is patience. You must be patient. I used to teach the concept "*people recover on their own time, not yours*", which meant that we needed to respect others for where they are and what they may need in that exact moment. They may need us to simply shut up and just listen. They may need ideas; they may need us to wait for them to figure it out on their own. Regardless of what they need at that moment we must practice patience to allow them the "*space*" to move through it.

Focused beliefs: It is vital that we have examined our own beliefs about others in general, as well as the individual themselves. We must realize that if we are already holding particular beliefs about a particular culture, ethnicity, gender, age, race, religion, sexual identity, political beliefs, financial position, social status, education, professional role, family history, etc. any one or all of them will impact the way we view an individual, and can surely impact our ability and/or willingness to intervene or assist a person in crisis. If we are at odds with the individual due to these beliefs it can and will distract us or even deter us from trying to help. It may hamper our ability to demonstrate care and concern for the person. Therefore, it is vital for us to examine ourselves regularly, and the ideas we have come to believe in regarding other people, and ensure we are not guilty of unfairly stereotyping a particular person, based on the actions of others.

Lastly, caring more than others deserve requires an attitude of gratitude. You must hold yourself to a higher standard, each and every day. It has been said that your attitude determines your altitude in life – thereby, you can directly direct your upward or downward path simply based on your attitude.

If you respond to a crisis situation with a negative, impatient, disrespectful, uncaring, or otherwise disingenuous attitude, you are headed towards trouble. The opposite being that by holding a positive mindset and attitude, your outlook and emotion of possibilities and potential can rub off on the other person in the crisis. Your outward expression of hope and positive energy can and will directly impact the other person and will challenge them to see the "*good*" or "*possibilities*" of the situation they face.

Einstein stated: "*There is no force in the universe strong enough to repel the power of a positive mind*". With that type of energy focused on an individual in need, how could they resist the temptation to a path of peace, and resolution?

**Law 2:**
Be the First to Try

---

When you are faced with a crisis, or a challenging situation, it is important that you are the "*first*" to move towards a solution. What this means is that you need to try and implement the first course of action to resolve the situation or provide an alternative to the individual that leads them to a better point in time.

For example: Asking permission to start over.

"*You are angry, and I can understand why*" "*Can we try and start over?*" or

"*You are frustrated, and I can definitely relate to that*"

"*Are you willing to let me try and help with this?*"

"*I understand you were hurt by what happened, and I can see why*"

"*I really want us to figure out how we can fix this, and try to move forward from here*"

People in crisis want to feel heard, we know this. They want to feel as though the other person is willing to work harder than them to "*come over*" first, so to speak. I know from personal experience, that it is really hard to start calming down "*first*" in an argument. The feeling that you are not going to give up any ground to the other person until they show that they are willing to "*give*" something is tough to overcome. For this reason, I encourage you as the responder to try and always be the first to "*try*".

Whether that means you try to better understand the person, or try harder to listen to their words, to try and bridge the gap between you, to try and relate, gain perspective, apologize, or put out your hand as a sign of vulnerability–there are so many ways to "*try*" and resolve the crisis, and if you are intent and focused on being the first to "*try*" and put in the effort, you will often discover that the method you use isn't as important as making the effort in and of itself. Individuals in crisis will likely see your efforts to try and find resolution and our human nature will demand that they either force themselves to deny it or grant it the respect that it deserves. Be the first to "*try*" in every difficult situation.

# The 15 Fundamental Laws of De-Escalation

**Law 3:**
Listen to What's Not Being Said

---

Of equal importance to what is being said, you must also pay great attention to what is **not** being said (*at least verbally*). There are many statistics and studies out there regarding body language, hand positions, stances, eye contact vs. no eye contact, etc. All of these things are critical to getting inside of the individual's mind during a crisis. Many persons in crisis cannot fully verbalize what they are feeling without extreme outbursts of emotion. Vulgar language can color the sentences and cloud the listening ability of the responder if they are not prepared or ready for such words. Tone of voice and inflection are very important when listening to the actual words that are said.

Do you hear stress in their voice—apart from the possible anger, do you hear tension or fear? Listening carefully and watching where the eyes are directed can also tell you quite a bit about the intentions of the person.

In law enforcement, they teach recruits to always be careful of the individual who keeps looking at your holstered weapon. If they are looking at it, it is likely they are considering getting ahold of it. You are taught to adjust your stance, or "*get off the X*" (*meaning that you need to quickly move from that spot*) as the individual may be triangulating on that location to lunge. By moving to a new spot, the mind is briefly delayed and/or thrown off and has to readjust the plan. This can buy you time and distance when needed.

Paying attention to the eyes of someone you are talking to, can provide you with a lot of information as well. Are they looking directly into your eyes? Are they avoiding eye contact? Direct eye contact can demonstrate intensity and focused energy. Avoidance of eye contact can mean distraction, or discomfort with the words being said. It may also be a cultural sign of respect NOT to look you in the eye, as it means to challenge or attempt to intimidate. Just as critical to watching the eyes of the individual, is being aware of the message that you send with yours. Be focused and intent with your gaze, though avoid using your eyes as a demonstration of power or intimidation as well. Recognize the importance of the eyes and the old adage "*the eyes are the windows to the soul*".

It is also important to avoid letting your mind lose its focus on the important points of the conversation. You may be tempted to preemptively provide an answer to a question or statement the individual is making, before they even ask it. This can not only demonstrate to the person that you are not fully listening, but can also show that you are not in tune with what isn't being said at that exact moment. Read between the lines, though you are not always correct to point out verbally what you see and believe early on in the conversation. The best therapists and counselors will advise you that most successful clients have "*figured out*" and worked through their own issues of struggle through discussion and verbally walking through the obstacles they face vs. **being told** what the solutions are. They are asked questions which guide them to thoughts they have not yet thought, or goals they have not yet set, or targets they have not yet identified. This first step in helping the individual is listening to both the words being said, as well as what is **not** being said.

**Law 4:**
Seek Harmony, Not Balance

---

When you engage in de-escalation with an individual in crisis, you should seek to find harmony, not balance.

Harmony = connection and ease of use

Harmony = engagement with purpose

Harmony = rapport without measurement

Balance = finding equality between weights and measure

Balance = attempting to ensure there is equal accountability and responsibility

Balance = a constant give and take of intelligent conversation

All of the things that balance is and represents are great when dealing with a person not in crisis. When dealing with a person who is not mentally unstable, or mentally ill. When dealing with a person that can hold calm and reasonable conversation.

Harmony is all the ways you can try to align yourself with something or someone, even when it is unbalanced.

Even when it is uncomfortable.

Millions of dollars are spent trying to teach people how to find balance in both their lives, thoughts and feelings.

We have all chased "balance" when in effect, what we needed was to locate harmony, and discover where and how we needed to grow or change in order to pull the sides of our lives and experiences together in a meaningful and effective way.

The path to find harmony can be seen in a simple exercise. Take your arms and stretch them in front of you, with palms facing you. Imagine two separate ideas, concepts, physical objects, etc. in each palm. Imagine the weight of one vs. the other. Imagine the temperature of one vs. the other. Imagine the texture of one vs. the other. In effect, when you are dealing with someone in crisis, and you are not in crisis, you are the polar opposite of that person.

They are likely fearful; you are likely calm. They are likely anxious or feel anger, you are less unsteady, and likely peaceful. They are red hot, you are "cool". They are forceful, you are flexible. They are powerful, you are measured. As a result, you remain opposites. The only way to come together is to find a way to harmonize.

Placing your hands palm to palm, while touching, you are still your own idea against their idea. One on top of the other and one person has dominance and one has submitted. One next to another, we are speaking the same language, but still from either side of the street.

The only way to come together and ensure both sides get to hold onto their ideas and emotions being safely protected and respected, is to align and harmonize together, and interweave between each other, to become two hands, clasped together, woven into one fist.

**Law 5:**
Two Vs. One

---

You must remember in any crisis situation that you were born with two ears, and only one mouth. You are meant to listen more than you speak. While we discussed the idea of listening for what is not being said, you must also strive to listen more, and talk less.

The most glaring place where this point has been made is in my personal life, in relationships. I am a problem solver. I think and create, and resolve, and move, and adapt, and overcome. I am constantly scanning; I am constantly seeking to pick up on changes in my environment and looking to resolve any confrontation near me. In the airport, in the grocery store, in the restaurant, in traffic, wherever I am, I am always on the alert for potential crisis, as it is my nature, my job, to resolve it. To fix it. To provide the answer; directly, immediately, clearly, and absolutely. In LE you are expected to immediately threat discriminate and mitigate the issue. Application of this tactic in my relationships, is an abject failure, 90% of the time.

She presents me with her "problem". Right away my mind kicks into gear seeking an immediate solution to her problem. It believes it has found an effective (if not the most effective) answer. That answer then immediately passes from the deep recesses of my mammalian brain (likely the amygdala--fight or flight discrimination is key at this point ☺) and into my cognitive brain and convinces my motor neurons to place the thought into words and immediately provide my partner with "the answer" which often sounds like "Well, I think you should….."

You readers will immediately recognize the problem with this situation. I have undoubtedly failed to listen to the complete situation, or "listen to what is not being said" and reacted too quickly with a verbal response. Rather than use my two ears to listen and ensure that I fully understand the situation before responding, I instead open my mouth to quite literally insert my entire foot, ankle, shin, calf, and knee.

As in any crisis de-escalation encounter, the amount in which you are listening is likely, not enough. You are most likely talking too much. You are very likely convincing yourself that you know the answer, and that if they would only listen to you, the situation would be resolved. It has long ago been established that persons in crisis most often simply wish to feel as though they have been "heard".

Above all else, as human beings, we want to be respected and listened to. If as a responder, we are failing to do this first task, we are far behind the eight-ball from the start. You don't have to worry about using the right technique, or finding the right phrase to use, etc. as you have yet to even fully "hear" the individual standing before you. By failing to actually hear them, you are not capable of finding an answer that is likely to work or resolve the issue for the long term. Sure, you may offer something that is somewhat of a temporary fix, but the individual has not fully expressed the emotion or thought and therefore it does one of two things:

One, it retreats back, goes into hiding and the person shuts down and determines that they are not "safe" to express themselves fully with you (which leads to all kinds of resentment and issues later)

Two, it causes them to retaliate at an even higher level of escalation as they do not feel respected or valued in the moment and are driven to operate from a "this person is a "threat" to me and my feelings" and therefore escalate out of a psychological need to defend or protect.

Both options are detrimental to the process of communication and de-escalation and can be prevented entirely, of just being an excellent listener and pausing before you respond, no matter what you even actually say. Even if your response is "wrong", you are being a great listener, which everyone truly wants to experience when they have emotions to share.

**Law 6:**
What You Think vs. What You Know

---

What do you know?!!! What do you know, King??! What do you know!!

I remember the police academy instructor yelling this at me over and over. Loud, forceful, aggressive. In my ear, behind me, while in a scenario-based training. I was tasked to handle the situation very quickly, and make a decision based on the information I had at that time. The information I had been given was very little.

"Man in the apartment building with a gun."

I am at the bottom of the stairs. The man is standing at the top of the apartment stairs, his side facing me, a handgun in his right hand, pointed slightly downward towards the landing front of him. He is not making any moves, nor saying anything. Just quiet, not yet appearing to know I am there, almost as if hiding in plain sight. I do not know if he is an undercover, a criminal, an armed citizen, under the influence, deaf, mute, etc.

I remember thinking to myself in that moment that I have to announce myself, (with gun drawn of course), call out to him and try to establish what he was doing, and determine what his intentions are, yet, I have nearly nothing other than what I can see and hear in that moment.

In those first few seconds I am supposed to figure out who he is, why he is there, what his intentions actually are, and consider if the gun is real, or even loaded. Essentially, is he a threat or not? The problem is I have no actual understanding as to the TOTALITY of the situation.

Quite often this is the same issue that arises when dealing with someone in crisis. We arrive on the scene or are in the room with the individual, and we enter that space (either physically or figuratively in our mind) and believe that we already understand what is going on. Time after time, crisis after crisis, I have seen this situation play out where the responder arrives with the idea that they already know what is going on and have selected a course of action. They then feign listening to the individual and attempt to demonstrate empathy for a few moments, all the while going over in their mind what they are going to say next, or even do next.

Now, keep in mind there is something I want you to enter into these situations with at the forefront of your mind (Law number 11 will address this in depth-"What's In It For Me?") though right now, in this initial few moments of contact with the individual your focus is safety, and keeping yourself and the individual as "safe" (physically and psychologically) as possible.

You should be concerned with nothing other than "Am I safe?" and "Are they safe?".

All of us want to avoid feeling threatened. I cannot listen, nor function at my highest levels if I am concerned for my safety, or uncomfortable in the physical surroundings. In the simplest of explanations, your brain and my brain escalates into a state of hyper-arousal in its efforts to protect our physical and psychological being. It places the majority of our thoughts and brain activity on "survival" activities.

Therefore, there is a lowered ability to reason, have complex thought patterns, and perform complex motor skills such as is needed during effective listening. All of these apply just the same for the individual I am seeking to de-escalate.

When you are speaking with someone, even if not extremely escalated (just in a Disagreement or Resistance Emotional Response Levels©) their brain is still scanning and listening for something that may be "threatening" on a physical or psychological level.

When you present yourself as either "all-knowing" or are "confrontational" to their world view (in that moment) due to thinking you already have all the answers to their issues without even have heard them out, you become a psychological threat to that individual. I have seen this process play out many times, when a responder makes up their mind about the individual in the first few seconds of the encounter, and instead of placing that perspective/judgement as something that may need to be altered or adjusted once the TOTALITY of the situation and circumstances are known, they stick to that first assessment. They refuse to change their attitude or feelings towards that person, even after hearing more of the facts surrounding it.

*Emotional Response Levels – CCG Crisis Escalation and De-escalation model*

"Ego" which I have heard referenced as "easing God out", takes over. Being "right" is more important than potentially recalibrating to the facts that are being made known and adjusting doesn't happen and both the individual in crisis feels more confrontational, and the responder refuses to back down.

"Man in the apartment building with a gun"

Turns out, I yell out to the man at the top of the stairs "Sheriff's Office!" "Drop the gun!!", he quickly stiffens, and freezes.

I get even louder with my commands "SHERIFF'S OFFICE!!" DROP THE GUN!" as I feel the rush of intensity building.

I don't want to get shot, and I don't want to fail the exercise.

He now turns his face to look at me, just his head.

I KNOW that the speed at which a person facing me with a gun pointed at the ground, can actually be brought up to eye level and fired at me, faster than I can squeeze the trigger of my gun already pointed at that individual. (This has been tested and empirically proven – See Force Science Institute® for more on this)

Action will always beat reaction.

Yet in this moment, I KNOW only his head is facing me. I KNOW that in order for him to take the shot, he has to turn around and make a major twisting movement with his upper body and arms, swinging the barrel of the gun around in my direction. Obscuring this action from my view is not possible. If he chooses to attempt that action, to try and turn around to shoot, I KNOW I will beat him to the trigger, and I will put him down. This I KNOW.

For this reason, I am able to hesitate and recalibrate, and seek to gain as much information about the situation as possible, as quickly as possible. I attempt to read the body language and facial expression that I can now see.

He is fearful. He is not aggressive. This could be a ploy. This could be real.

I again yell out, "DROP THE GUN, NOW!!" After what seems like an eternity, he does.

As the weapon begins to fall from his hand, he deliberately angles even more downward, in such a way that I can now see the bright red tip on the end of the barrel. (While this was a training evolution and I know we are using blue rubber training guns, we are told at the beginning to treat them as real weapons)

For this scenario, I now see that the instructors deliberately taped this one with red tape to simulate the toy-guns you see in the stores.

It was meant to be a toy gun for this "shoot-don't shoot" scenario.

I immediately feel a huge rush of relief, as I realized I didn't end up shooting a man with a toy gun.

The man says to me "Ok, ok, please, please…!!" "Don't shoot, don't shoot!" "I'm just playing cops and robbers with my kids" "I was trying to sneak up on them!" "It's fake, it's fake!!"

The scenario ends shortly after and I breathe a few more sighs of relief. The instructor says, "Good job King."

"You had limited information. You of course had your belief about what you were facing and dealt with it the right way." "Though instead of making an instant decision based on very little information, you gathered more information in just a few more seconds on what you were facing and made a different decision than many others have." "We deliberately placed you in that location, at the bottom of the steps, with limited information." "Many others to come through have used these few circumstances to justify taking the shot right away." "You did not, good job." While shoot/no-shoot decision making is not the same as choosing to pre-judge someone who is simply upset and/or challenging you on a topic, the results can be just as critical. Do everything you can to weigh out all the facts before you make a decision. Consider you don't know everything. Safety first, then open yourself to consider there is more than just your perspective on the situation. Think back to other times in your life when you "just knew" everything about a thing, and without a doubt were right, only to later realize (either on your own or someone else telling you) that you were incorrect, and really missed the boat. I heard not long ago, that when you find yourself saying "I know all about this" you likely only know about 50% of all there is to know on it, as you have already convinced yourself that you know all there is on it, and are closed off to learning more.

**Law 7:**
Raise Your EQ

---

One of the most critical and Fundamental Laws of De-escalation, is the understanding that you must have in regard to raising your Emotional Intelligence (EQ or EI).

If I had the power to completely rewrite the accreditation guides for Joint Commission, CARF and various other Best Practices found in the industry, in relation to crisis prevention and intervention training, this would be where it starts.

I truly believe that if you are NOT emotionally intelligent, you will fail the majority of the time when attempting to de-escalate someone in crisis. I believe this so strongly that I speak to it in every training course we provide. I actually have an online course where I teach how EQ functions into crisis prevention.

EQ has been considered to have 5 different components, all of which are critical. I will give a brief outline here, though it isn't a complete explanation, just some major points.

1. **Self-Awareness** – As has been mentioned elsewhere and many training manuals of the past, having a real understanding of who you are, and what you "bring" to a situation is vital. Are you projecting the image and demeanor you wish to present? Are you conscious of how you speak? The tone you use? The affect you have? What others feel when you enter a room? What you look like? What are your values? What are your boundaries? What areas do you consider sacred when in conversation? Where are the lines drawn when those you are speaking to get escalated? Are you a good listener? Are you a great

listener? Do you engender trust from others? Are you likeable? Are you confident without being cocky? Are you in tune with your own body, mind, and spirit so that you are in congruence when you are interacting with others? Do you know how to express yourself honestly, without condemning others or hurting others' feelings (to the extent that you can influence that)? The list can go on and on, but you must have a baseline of understanding yourself, or you are headed for trouble.

2. **Self-Regulation** – Quite simply the question is: Are you able to control yourself and your behavior when under extreme stress? So often, crisis situations play out in the media or other public areas in stages that are clearly visible to those watching, or after the fact, but not to the responder in the moment. You can often see the exact moment where the responder's buttons get pushed. They stiffen, either physically or psychologically, and you can see and hear the change. They now lose the ability to remain neutral and indifferent. Voices raise, questions turn to challenges, directions become threats, and it goes from there. A responder that has strong self-awareness feels themselves escalating, and similar to the process outlined in the great novel "The 5 Agreements" they are able to separate themselves from themselves. They can see themselves actually growing angry or escalated and are able to step back. They separate from the building emotions and don't allow them to actually direct or guide their behavior. As a result, they are not connected to the emotion of the moment (at least the negative) and are calmly able to continue to listen, recalibrate, and re-engage successfully with the person in crisis. If we all seek to remember to try and do this

when we feel ourselves getting challenged emotionally, we will be far ahead of the game.

3. **Motivation** – Another key component to the process is the concept of motivation and having it focused on resolution. I believe that if a responder is truly able to connect to the "why" behind why they are there, the importance of the "job" they have at that exact moment (whether professional or personal), they will be successful at de-escalation. If someone tasked with helping others during crisis who may be very "venomous" or hurtful with their words and behavior, and the responder cannot connect with their inner motivation to demonstrate patience, tolerance, or otherwise positive to the individual, they headed for trouble. I will always encourage you to remember a great perspective, attributed to Viktor Frankl, Author, PhD, and Holocaust Survivor "When you know your why, you can endure any how". When it comes to crisis de-escalation, I encourage you to find and discover your "why", which will give birth, and rebirth to your motivation to actually do it.

4. **Empathy** – This has been described as the ability to understand, relate, connect, share or otherwise comprehend another's feelings, perspective, or thoughts. This is fairly self-explanatory I believe. Can you find the space for someone else's feelings or thoughts on a subject, especially when it is something that they tell you is difficult for them to endure? I spent countless hundreds of hours working with persons that wanted to commit suicide and could see no other way out. Whether it was with teens in the hospital, despondent husbands or wives on their way to jail working in law

enforcement, fellow veterans after we got back from the war, or even friends that just were feeling completely overwhelmed. One of the biggest gifts I had for them in that situation, was expressing my own path down the road towards my own suicide attempt. When they heard that I too, had felt such hopelessness and desperation, it created a bond and connection to work from. The issue though, is when you haven't had a similar experience to the one that is being shared with you by the person in crisis. What if you have never experienced what they are going through and they know it? Maybe by simply the nature of what it is, it's not possible for you to have gone through it. How do you in that moment find the "space" within yourself to have empathy? I believe that one of the easiest ways to do so, is to become humble and lead with humility. Tell the person that you don't exactly know what it must be like for them, but you want to try and understand. Ask them to tell you and explain it so that you can better understand. If the individual is willing to actually express it, and you are in the right mindset, you can surely then go back into your own recollection and find a situation that is likely to relate, and thereby you can find that connection to what they are feeling. If you can do that, then you can demonstrate an empathetic response that is likely helpful to getting them to de-escalate, at least a bit more.

5. **Social Skill** – This last component, I do believe can be the trickiest. Some of you reading this, will simply just suck at this. You just will. If you are not normally someone who is a "chameleon" or an extrovert, or someone who enjoys being around other people, you

may have a very difficult time with this. Reason being is that connecting and building relationship and rapport with people during crisis is not something that is always clear and step-by-step. Its fluid. You must be able to "go with the flow" of the situation as it often will rapidly change. As been mentioned in the past, you may be headed down one direction in a crisis and the individual decides to completely go down a different "road", and you must be able to adjust. You must be able to gently shift into that next point of conversation without forcing them to return to a stuck point. It may be that they want to shift to avoid dealing with or talking about a particular issue, which may be cause to try and shift them back if necessary; though you must be able to do it with finesse. If you know this is something you are good at, then you got it. If you know right now, this isn't you, then I would suggest you take up additional learning on basic communication and seeking to improve the way you engage with others and share your ideas, as they share theirs.

To sum up this chapter, EQ is something you can definitely improve if you so choose. Use the 5 components to your advantage and build on each section as elements of your personality and who you can become overall as you move through life. Increased EQ will absolutely improve your ability to de-escalate crisis situations. No question.

## Law 8:
## Separate Yourself From It

One of the most difficult, yet powerful tools you can develop in your de-escalation arsenal is to learn to separate yourself from the potential emotional rise that the words they use, or actions they are taking. Easier said than done; I know.

In looking back on my past experience working with people in crisis while in professional roles (a cop, a probation officer, a psych tech, mental health worker, etc.) I was truly phenomenal at "separating myself". My ability to predict a potential crisis, intervene, mitigate, and resolve it in those environments was fantastic.

Personal situations and relationships though, are another story. Let's just say it's a work in progress, that needs a constant ton of work. ☺

I have learned in the last few years especially, that when my personal feelings are involved, my ability to remain detached or separated from the emotions rising to the surface, is very difficult for me. At times it feels near impossible. So, this begs the question: Why?

The easiest answer I can think of is that when I am speaking to someone "professionally" they don't really "know me" and therefore can't "hurt me" with what they say. As long as I choose not to give their words, actions, or perspectives about or towards me the credibility to impact what I think about myself in that moment, I'm good. But that's the easy answer.

Why is it that I have found this to be the case with so many folks that work in the field? They are fantastic at work, but terrible at home. They are fantastic at home, and at work, things get under their skin, and they escalate. In my experience there have been very few who are equally strong in both arenas. Many of those that I have met are either very spiritual beings, or persons that just simply have an attitude that follows them throughout everything they do, of peace and love. Many of them had dreadlocks. Not kidding. It's just something about the total mind body heart connection that they held where they were able to remain grounded in themselves and the moment without allowing anything that was going on around them to escalate them from the state they were in to begin with.

Another resource I came across recently offer the advice of considering "SAD HATS"* as if you or someone you are dealing with is in any of these conditions it tends to put that person into what is considering the "primitive brain" and therefore may make escalation more likely.

S – is for Sick

A – is for Alcohol

D – is for Drugs

H – is for Hungry

A – is for Anxiety

T – is for Tired

S – is for Stress

I would encourage you to always be very aware of being in any of the above states and evaluate if it is impacting your own ability to remain detached from the crisis/behavior that you are being faced with. Consider for a moment the last time you were sick—were you truly in the best headspace to be told that something you are doing was "wrong" or "out of control" or "causing a scene" or otherwise in need of changing? I know that when hungry, I am much quicker to become stressed and more impatient. If we take this one step further and consider that the person you are dealing with is very likely in one of the above conditions, and is therefore acting "under the influence" you may find it easier to separate yourself from the emotions that are rising within you, as you recognize they are not truly acting in their best state.

As a final consideration, there surely may be situations where you need to physically remove yourself from the situation altogether as you just simply need to be allowed to get away from potential toxicity. While there isn't always an easy way to step away, there are surely ways to do so that are destructive or traumatic to the person in crisis. One of the most powerful things you can do is advise the person that you would like to take few minutes to think about what they said and seek to better understand how they feel. While you may be stepping away for other reasons, it provides a solid base to work from which most persons in crisis won't argue with it. They likely now believe you will possibly become convinced of their situation, feelings, or emotions as being "right" when you return. Regardless if you do or not, it allows the space for both persons to de-escalate just by reducing the tension of proximity.

(*Crisis Intervention Certification Handbook, by Andrew Prisco, CCIS-V, Laura Moss, CCIS-IV, Rich Pfeiffer, Ph.D.)

**Law 9.**
Friendly, But Not Friends

---

"No greater friend, no worse enemy" Gen. Mattis – USMC

General Mattis visited my Battalion when I was in Iraq in 2003 with the 4th Light Armored Reconnaissance Btn. It was during that year when he made that great quote in reference to how us Marines were to treat the Iraqi's. To let them know that we would be their greatest friend should they seek friendship and cooperation, yet if they sought to cause us harm, or kill us—we ought to be their worst enemy imaginable.

Looking back, it was war. It was not a fun experience or time, yet one I remember with honor and gratitude for the opportunity to serve what I thought was a noble cause and support my fellow Marines.

The quote from the General reminds me of the chapter title, which was told to me by one of my first supervisors when I was working with youth at the substance abuse treatment center. I was brand new, just 19 years old and doing my best to learn quickly how to navigate the dynamics at work being just over 2 years sober and having been a patient there myself, at that exact facility.

"Brendan, you are here to be friendly, but not their friend". At first, I really resented the advice. I felt like he had it all wrong. That in fact the key to building a relationship with the youth there was being exactly that, a friend. I knew what it was to be hurting like they were. Alone like they felt. Broken on the inside like they shared. The very thing I wanted back then was a "friend"---or so I thought.

It took me a few years to really understand what it was he was saying. He was pointing out that I really didn't recover myself because the staff there became my "friend". I recovered because I was surrounded by people who were willing to risk hurting my feelings, stressing me out, pressing my buttons (therapeutically), and more to ensure that I could walk out of there one day on my own, and stay clean. Had they instead been overly concerned about my liking them or counting on them to always listen to all my whining, and complaining, or attempt to give me a solution to my problems like a good friend always does, I wouldn't have made it. Instead they kept professional distance and were more so guiding me like a mentor or coach would, to dig deep and find my own footing. To build my own foundation beneath me. A friend offers to reach down into the pit and lift you up. What it was going to take for me to get through those times was them handing me a shovel, so I could dig steps into the sides of my pit and climb up and out on my own.

I'd ask you to consider this concept during your next crisis encounter. Consider that you don't have to break your own emotional, psychological, or of course physical boundaries or limits in order to help someone, but instead give them the tools that they don't already have. The tools necessary that they can use to get back on the right side of the situation.

These may be simple tools, like actively listening to them without providing the answer. It may be encouraging them to think back to another time when they had to "pull through" in a similar way. It may be letting them know that you hear them and can understand why they feel the way they do, and that its ok, and stopping before you try to make them feel better. It may be encouraging them to take a break, a time out away from something toxic. It may be sharing about something you went through in your life that was difficult even though it may not be the exact same thing, just so they know everyone has had struggles, without giving away so much detail that they can use it against you in the future.

Your goal is to simply be friendly and help them find their way back to calm, from crisis. Getting to a point where you are giving them your contact information to reach out to you anytime they are struggling, is very likely, exactly the wrong thing to do. If you find that you are feeling inclined to do so with many crisis situations you are dealing with, you ought to take a solid look at what your deep motivations actually are and get clear.

## Law 10.
## Actually, Not Everyone Is F%^ked Up

---

When working with individuals in crisis we have to remember that there are more "good" people than "bad". It's very possible that the person you are dealing with may seem to be so out of control and escalated, that they appear to be possessed by the devil. If you are able to hold onto the thought that the person you are trying to help is not truly a "bad" person, they likely are just having a "bad" day, you will be ahead of the game.

Everyone you come in contact with is unique. You may have dealt with the same type of crisis 1000 times over, and sometimes even with the same person, yet each time has the potential to be different. It has the same potential to end up differently, either positively, or negatively, with the influence being stronger from the responder to go either way as we have discussed. Keeping all of that in mind, it's also very important to do all you can to avoid becoming "jaded" and preconditioned to label or become prejudiced to those you may encounter based on your past experience, no matter how many years of it you have.

During my years spent working in locked psychiatric treatment facilities, my first few years were spent on a children's mental health unit with kids 5yrs old and under. Over time, somewhat unconsciously, I began to think that all kids in that age group must behave and act like the ones in my care. Day in and day out, dealing with the kids' issues, over 40 hours a week makes an impact. Keep in mind, the kids that were in the facility were nearly 90% all victims of horrible abuse, neglect, or similar trauma. The screaming, yelling, fighting, crying, throwing things, punching, biting, etc. combined with the constant sadness, depression, hopelessness, loneliness, anxiousness, and fearful behavior soon became the norm. To have a kid try to hurt me, or another staff or child was daily. To have kids hurt themselves via self-harm (cutting/scratching/banging head/punching walls, etc.) was a near hourly occurrence. It was very, very difficult to work there. Within about 6 months or so I came to believe that it was nearly impossible to think that any kid could actually behave or actually be happy.

A few years later, I was regularly being asked to speak at public schools to young students about drug abuse and the dangerous of at-risk behavior. On one occasion, when I was leaving an elementary school after an event, I remember seeing some of the students getting on buses to go home for the day. I distinctly remember hearing them giggling, laughing, etc. and seeing them smile as they played games waiting for their buses to be called. They were actually laughing out loud, smiling and joking, and seemed truly happy. I remember thinking to myself in those few minutes that something was wrong. I was uncomfortable. Something bad was about to happen, and I was just standing there poised and ready to intervene.

Slowly then, as the minutes passed with nothing happening, I slowly grew calmer and more comfortable. I began to realize that there was actually nothing wrong. Nothing bad was going to happen. I could "stand down."

It was exactly as it was supposed to be.

This was "normal", and it was ok.

I then became so overwhelmed by what I was hearing and seeing, I became tearful and broke down crying. I started towards my car.

It was at that moment that I realized that I had truly forgotten what "normal" or "well-adjusted" was. I hadn't realized just how deeply working in that environment had affected me, and how hardened and disheartened I had become.

Simultaneously, it was in those same moments that I was gracefully reminded why I was doing the work I was doing. Why I continue to teach and lead my company to provide the safest and most effective Crisis Prevention & Intervention Training® around the globe today.

It was, and still is my passion to help make sure children, adolescents, and adults can return to a life filled with joy, happiness, and laughter after potentially living a life of hell prior to.

## The 15 Fundamental Laws of De-Escalation

**Law 11:**
What's in It for Me?

---

As the first action step of the 5-Steps of De-escalation, the most important concept is to consider where you are internally, emotionally and psychologically before you even begin dealing with the crisis situation, reason being is that the most pivotal person in a crisis is the responder. Individuals that are in crisis are quite often the most predictable persons during an event. Reason being is that we have all witnessed individuals in crisis, and the behavior that they exhibit. It is loud, predictable, and something that can be mitigated with cautious skills. We can relate to anger. We can relate to frustration with things in our lives. We can relate to sadness and guilt or fear over a particular situation, which is very likely the same thing the individual in crisis is struggling with.

This all said, the most critical aspect to understanding the 5 Steps of De-escalation is recognizing that we ourselves, must master our own mindset, and thought patterns FIRST, long before we can expect to be successful at de-escalating someone else in crisis. As I have taught for years, if you start your day in a state of mind that is in conflict with someone, or something, you are already at a disadvantage when facing someone in crisis. You are in our own struggle to find harmony in your mind, you are in your own space of struggle. Same concept of how a drowning person cannot save another drowning person. You will only pull the other person down with you as you both claw for the surface to find your way out.

Consider the situation of heading out for work in the morning and you are off your "game".

You have spilled coffee on your shirt in the car;

Which was due to the fact that you had to race out the door;

Because you were slowed up by having to clean up the cat puke on the floor;

Which was after you had to reset the fuse in the garage,

Which you had to do in order to get the hot water working;

Since the storm last night somehow tripped the breaker;

Which also had caused the circuit in the kitchen to as well so you your pre-brewed coffee that was supposed to be ready, wasn't,

Which to add on top of that was yet another reason you should have just sprung for the Keurig like your wife kept saying you should;

Which was not something you had wanted to do, because it just doesn't't make sense to pay over $130 for a cup of coffee.

So, for these reasons, the first customer, patient, or other human being you encounter who has an "issue" with their own life, just doesn't't seem like something you can force yourself to care about at this time.

Being that law #1 Is to Care More Than Others Deserve, you are screwed at the start.

Finding a solution will likely come from creating a process that you do every morning which gets you in the right state of mind. Over the years I have tried very hard to position myself in the right state of mind every morning--quite frankly

## The 15 Fundamental Laws of De-Escalation

I was often able to do so subconsciously due to my overall drive and determination to provide for my family and myself, and grow my company day after day, week after week, year after year. That said, the fire slowly dies out over time and the need to find myself a real routine became critical. I recently started a new pattern which has worked amazingly. It's called the Core 4 which I learned from a program called Wake Up Warrior, and genius entrepreneur and thought leader, Garret J White.

It begins at 5am every day. Every day. No breaks for weekends, no breaks on holidays. Every day you #DTFW (Do The F****ing Work). Like breathing. I wake up at 5:00am. I immediately break a quick sweat through some kind of physical activity. Usually for me, it is 50 air squats. You don't have to get a huge workout in right then, it's just about blood flow. It is enough movement to get the heart and blood pumping and fully "wake" me up. I then drink a green smoothie which I prepared the night before (85-90% green veggies and carrots, with just a bit of fruit for taste). I then get the coffee ready. I then use the headspace app and meditate for at least 15 minutes. Next, I journal for another 10-15 to get the brain working on a positive flow from the start. I then listen to something (podcast/audible/video) that teaches me something I didn't already know. I then make my declaration for the day. Something that motivates me to push forward and focus on a specific target for the day. I then spend another few minutes writing sticky notes to each of my kids and wife which I place on their bathroom mirrors to encourage them as soon as they wake up in the am. I share some of that "energy" that I have already received myself through this morning routine. This all happens before 6 am. This process has changed my life. If you are open to this process, trust me, it will change yours as well. (Learn more about this at www.wakeupwarrior.com or www.wakeupwarriorwomen.com ).

With the C4, I have MORE energy throughout the day. I have MORE peace. I have MORE serenity. I have MORE drive than ever before. I have MORE clarity in my decisions and thought patterns. I have CERTAINTY in where I am going and what I will achieve, not only in the day, but in my life.

Without starting off focused on putting myself above everyone and everything else, I have nothing to give to others. Though I may be offering up some of what is inside me, the reality is that without fueling up in the morning on the positive energy I need for me, I run dry giving to others. Make the decision to put yourself first. "Core 4 before I hit the door". Stake your claim in yourself first, every freaking day.

Ensuring that you are taking care of yourself, every morning, every single day, you are at an optimum level to handle and be strong enough to absorb more positive energy and repel the negative that comes your way.

This is a non-negotiable when it comes to de-escalation. You have to be mindful of your own condition (as explained before) or you are entering into the crisis cycle with another individual at a severe disadvantage. If you truly wish to be successful and get the most from your day and life in general, you must set this pattern into motion immediately.

**Law 12:**
Demonstrate No Threat

---

A lesson that I learned very early on, is that there is always someone bigger, faster, stronger, meaner. Always. You may think that your ability to swell up and get loud, get aggressive, get challenging, etc. is a key to manage crisis situations– yet, you are wrong. Sun Tzu said – the mark of a true warrior is the ability to fight without fighting. Your goal in the confrontation is to avoid appearing as though you are a threat. You may be a spider monkey ninja like me on the inside, but on the outside, you need to appear calm, relaxed and in many ways, docile. There is a difference between appearing docile and calm, vs. weak and fearful. It is very possible to demonstrate no threat without appearing weak or vulnerable. You simply have to master the art of knowing yourself and your capabilities and recognize the strengths you do have beyond the physical or psychological.

Take a moment to consider yourself at your toughest, most ferocious moment. What do you see? What animal most represents who you would be? A wolf? A bear? A silverback gorilla? A cobra? A wolverine? A shark? A tiger? A hyena? A cat? All of these animals' hunt and are able to do so quite efficiently. That said, they all have the ability to use stealth, and hide their power and ability until they need it most.

Your goal is to have the strength and power to survive any encounter with confidence and calm demeanor, vs having a loud, aggressive or even obnoxious display. Use stealth in your communication. Use your ability to conceal and maintain your emotion as the gift to offer respite and resolution to the other individual you are dealing with in that moment. Your goal is to appear as though you are of no threat to the individual, only a resource to help them solve whatever situation is ailing them in that moment. You are the ferryman across the dark, fog-covered lake. You are only there to lead them to the other side.

One of the best stories I have of this entire 5 step process you are now reading is available in video form, if interested. I literally walk you through the encounter where I utilized this technique with an individual who was drunk and had wrecked his car. I had been dispatched to the scene while working in law enforcement, and he started the conversation towards me with "F**K YOU PIG!" the moment I arrived on scene and stepped out of my cruiser. It was great. To check it out, go to our website (calmeverystorm.com) and search for the course "5 Steps to De-escalation" in our options of online training.

The idea of demonstrating no threat goes against some types of training programs where they focus a large amount on "tactical presence" or using a "show of force" "controlling the x", etc. Trust me, I understand that there are times when this is necessary. Sadly, though, 9 times out of 10, that demonstration of threat is used at the wrong time.

As has been said, "with great power comes great responsibility". Especially when working in Law Enforcement, there is a great power and authority that is placed in the hands of each and every officer. Knowing when to use that power and wielding it at the right time is not easy, nor something that can come naturally to you in that moment. You may say ok BK, that makes sense and is easy for you to say when you have a badge and gun, Taser®, etc. You have tools on your belt to protect you. How do you practice this without having all those things?

I would present you with this argument. I have to work harder than you when in that situation. It is those exact tools and uniform that make me more of a threat to the individual, which I have to go above and beyond with them to try and present a reasonable, calm, and non-threatening person. So, touché'. We both have our work cut out for us. ☺

I want you to take some time thinking, meditating even on what you want to be seen as the next time crisis strikes. Would you like to be seen as the instigator? The enforcer? The friend? The ignorer? The mediator? The listener? The liar? The promiser? The fixer? Or simply, the solution? You have the opportunity to be any of these persons above and more, though there is one that I want you to truly go after. Being a "solution" doesn't mean you gave in, or gave up. It doesn't mean you won, or they lost. It simply means you resolved the crisis, no matter what it took. And you did so successfully.

## Law 13:
## Find An In

At the entrance to the de-escalation process is another vital component that must be considered in order to engage and connect with the individual in crisis. This is the next step in the process, which is "Find An In".

When meeting an individual where they are in that moment of escalation, the common characteristic they have is to try and create distance between themselves and those around them. If we can locate a place within us where we feel apart from, different, disadvantaged, less than or even greater than the other person we are focused on, we can escalate more easily. We can allow our anger or rage to flow out of us unencumbered by any "connection" we feel to the individual there with us.

One of the first tactics a hostage negotiator will use is to try and find a "connection" to the hostage taker. They will seek to discover and use some sort of "common ground" that they can relate to, or empathize with, similar to the bad actor. In this way, they then use that connection to their advantage to try and bond with them and gain more information. The greatest tool a negotiator has is time. Time that they can stall the progress of the incident and try and prevent some sort of harmful act being taken. Finding a common ground position to take can help create conversation between them and start the resolution of the event.

This is the same concept that is required during de-escalation of even minor disagreements. The responder needs to find a way to shorten the gap between themselves and the individual in crisis so they can start building the bridge towards connection and return to "we" vs. "me". One of the easiest ways to do so is to take a quick visual scan of the person and see what physical attributes they share in common or could be considered something to mention. For example, I shave my head clean with a razor about one time every 4 days or so. I have done so pretty much since returning from the war in Iraq. Keeping my hair short (where I can't even style or brush it) is the easiest. My wife says its necessary for my growing bald spot—who knows. Using this as a tool is easy. If I happen to be dealing with someone who is also bald, I may immediately throw in a comment early in the crisis like "Man... I see we have the same barber" This may be just enough to create a short break in the thought pattern of the person in crisis and lift the mood a bit. The other option may be if I see that they have a full head of hair, I may say to them, "Man, I just gotta say, I wish I had a full mane like you do", while stroking my hand across the top of my head and looking at their head with a jealous look on my face. Once again, a simple way to try and lighten the mood, and use that as a way to connect and "Find An In".

Another great tool is to actually use certain "helper" language with the individual like "I really would like to help you with this, are you willing to let me try?" Stated clearly and with conviction may demonstrate your empathy for the person and their situation which may provide you with a moment of connection with them. "I can completely understand why this would make you angry; I want to help figure out how we can fix it" When you use phrases that use the word help, and essentially express to this person that you are trying to help them through some type of circumstance they are in, it is quite difficult to argue with that. This doesn't mean that these sentences will work on an individual who is past the point of no return in the crisis cycle, but many times it will. You must become practiced at using these techniques as it is not only the concept of trying to "find the in", but using it at the right time and in the right manner can work wonders. Remember "Find An In".

**Law 14:**
Meet A Need

---

After you have found an in, your primary focus should be shifted to figuring out how to meet a need that the individual has in that moment. Are they thirsty? Fatigued? Do they want to sit down? Do they need space? Do they need help figuring out the next step? Do they need to feel safe? Do they have a question that needs to be answered? Do they want help to communicate what they are feeling/needing? Do they need assistance to get somewhere? What is it that they need, emotionally, physically, psychologically, etc.?

When you consider Maslow's Hierarchy of Needs you should focus on making sure the basic needs are met in the moment if possible. The fundamentals --- food, water, shelter (as applicable to the situation). Next, they must be kept safe, feel as though they are "safe". Next they need connection and empathy, grounding. After these needs are being met, your likelihood of them being in the right state of mind to perform complex motor skills such as thinking and communicating, can occur.

If they are stuck in fight or flight, they are not capable or able to logically communicate with you. Their primal brain has hijacked their mammalian brain and they are only trying to determine threat/no threat.

Standing there telling them to calm down, take a deep breath, or tell you what is bothering them is about as effective as telling a charging silverback gorilla to hold on one second. They are literally fighting in that moment for survival. Be it physical or psychological. You must determine how to get them beyond the fear, and uncertainty by using the prior steps in the process, to now be able to ask, and get an effective answer to how you can help them (i.e. meet a need).

You may be met with an impossible "ask". They may tell you in that moment that they must have something that you know to be impossible. This often has responders quite confused and perplexed. They have now asked the individual what they want, and they have gotten an answer, though now the answer is not something they can provide. They get stuck. If you have done a proper job of the prior steps, the connection that was gained in the prior step can be drawn upon to elicit potential empathy from the individual seeking the "thing". I would say something to the effect of; "Wow, John, that is a big ASK man. I think we both know my boss isn't going to let me do that" "Let's start with something easy first, and that way we can show you that we are going to stick to our word, and then you can show us you will too.." "This way, we can work up to something that may be harder to get"

Something of that nature should surely help get the point across that you are trying to work with them, though you don't have to confront the ask straight out with a "no, you can't, etc." or get stuck doing nothing.

**Law 15:**
Provide Options

---

The last step in this process is to "Provide Options". These are meant to be options that will work for the given situation. These may not be the long-term solution to the entire situation, but they will work right now. Right now, and in the next few moments are truly what is most important. You truly must focus on the here and now.

Be here, NOW.

So often, we find ourselves trying to solve all the problems that may arise at any time in the future. We can easily get caught up in thinking that while the individual may cooperate with you right now, they won't in the long term.

THIS DOES NOT MATTER RIGHT NOW!

If this situation you are facing is truly a "crisis" then the most important factor to consider is if the individual is going to de-escalate in this moment. Every moment you can influence the individual to take just one more moment without aggressive action, or violence, you are winning the long game. Take stock in finding the solution that works, right now, for both of you.

In mental health settings, this may require that you become flexible in your "rules" for the moment. Little Johnny refusing to stop screaming and throwing things unless he gets a snack before bed, may require bending in the moment for safety, and ensuring that appropriate consequences are applied in the morning. Too often staff focus on the "NO" to the right now, vs. the "How" in the future.

In Law Enforcement this isn't always as easy, but every officer ALWAYS has the ability to use their discretion and determine what is the safest and most important action to take, right now. This may mean not going "hands on" right this second, but instead allow the individual to sit down, step back, or similarly take a "time out" before rushing to get physical. It may simply be just 20-30 more seconds of patience that will result in coming up with an option that works in the short term to prevent further escalation.

Remember the 3 C's:

**Cooperation** vs Confrontation

**Coordination** vs. Control?

**Communication** vs. Criticism

Staying focused on the immediate win, in the here and now, that serve BOTH yourself and the individual in crisis are most important. There is a balance between providing options as solutions, or "giving in" as others may see it. Go macro. Think big picture. Think overall goal. Think possibility. A mentor of mine is well known to always use the following statement when asking someone to expand their mind and be open to a different perspective. The question he poses is, "I'd ask you to consider….."

To me, it is one of the most powerful questions you could pose to someone in crisis, or in any discussion to be honest.

First; you are "asking" for something, not telling them what to do.

Secondly; you identify that the question is directed it at them, and there can be no question as to who is in fact being asked to consider an alternative.

Thirdly; you are doubling down on the "ask", by inviting them to be open minded to what you are going to propose.

If you truly re-read the question multiple times, say it out loud, practice it and make it a regular part of your language, I guarantee you will be far more successful in even the most challenging crisis situations you encounter.

## In Conclusion

This last tip goes towards making the point that sometimes you need to know when to quit. When you are finishing up an intervention, a type of crisis situation that you de-escalated successfully, lay the groundwork for the next time. Choose something like, "You know John, I'm really glad we were able to work this out. You know, I hope if something comes up like this again, you and I will be able to work it out just like we did this time." This can truly be the beginning of an amazing connection with the individual especially when you know you will see them again. Do everything you can, to make the very last words you have with the individual positive ones. Therefore, in the same spirit;

*"I really hope you enjoyed reading this book and that you got something out of it. If willing, I'd ask you to consider reading my next one?"* ☺


Stay Safe, and Change Lives,

Brendan King

Crisis Consultant Group. (www.CrisisConsultantGroup.com)

EntreHow (www.EntreHow.com)

RISE – Ruthless Integrity & Simple Execution (www.RiseToRule.com)


You know what would be really amazing? I would love to hear from you and what (if anything) you felt you learned from this book, or enjoyed the most!

Please shoot me an email and let me know!
Brendan.King@crisisconsultantgroup.com